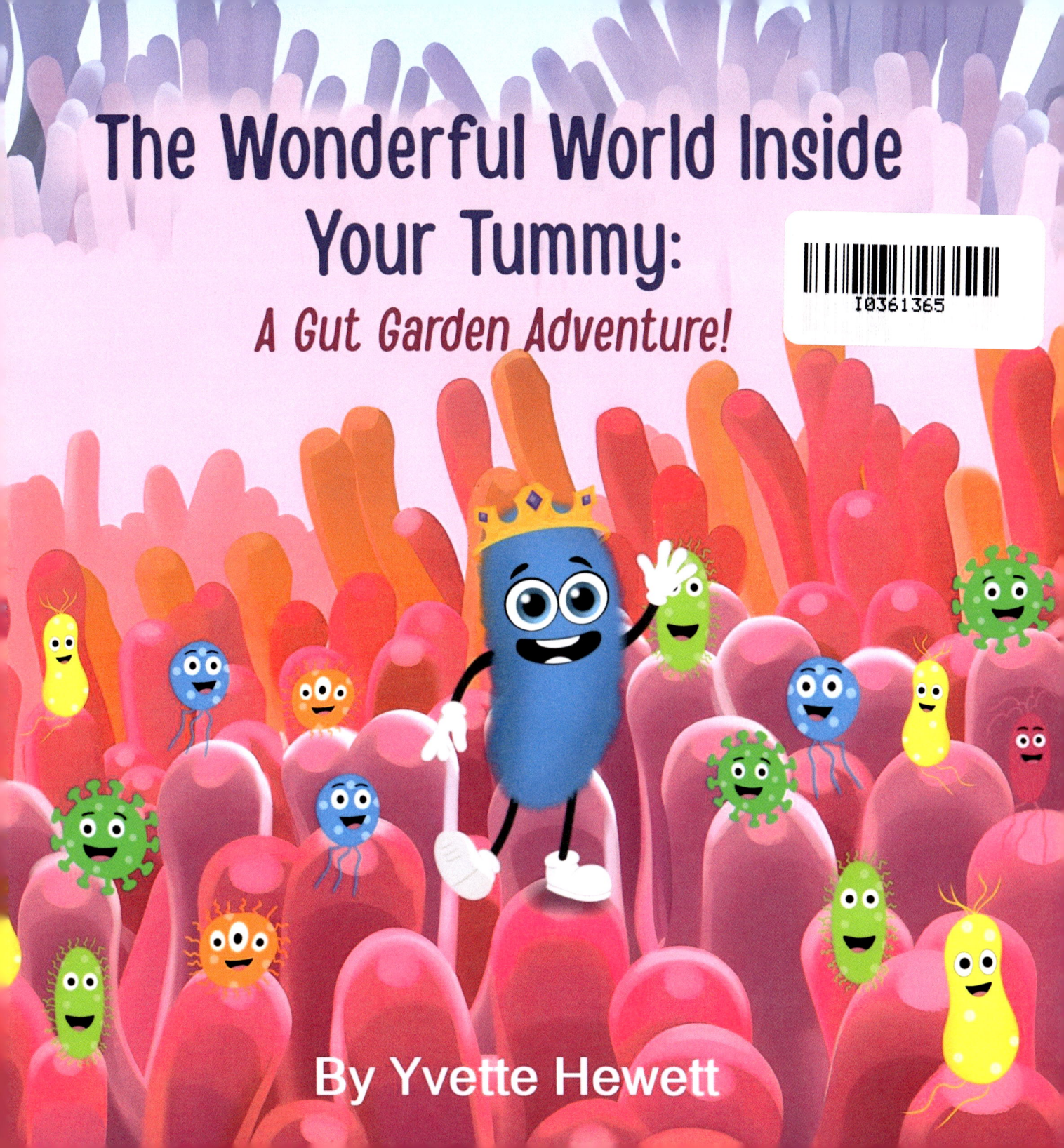

Copyright © 2024 Yvette Hewett
All rights reserved.
ISBN: 9798323649464

DEDICATION

To all the young adventurers exploring the marvelous world of guts and greens, may this book be your compass on the tasty journey to a happy, healthy belly! Here's to giggles, grins, and good gut feelings!

In a land far away (but actually very close - right inside your tummy!), lives a tiny adventurer named Pip.

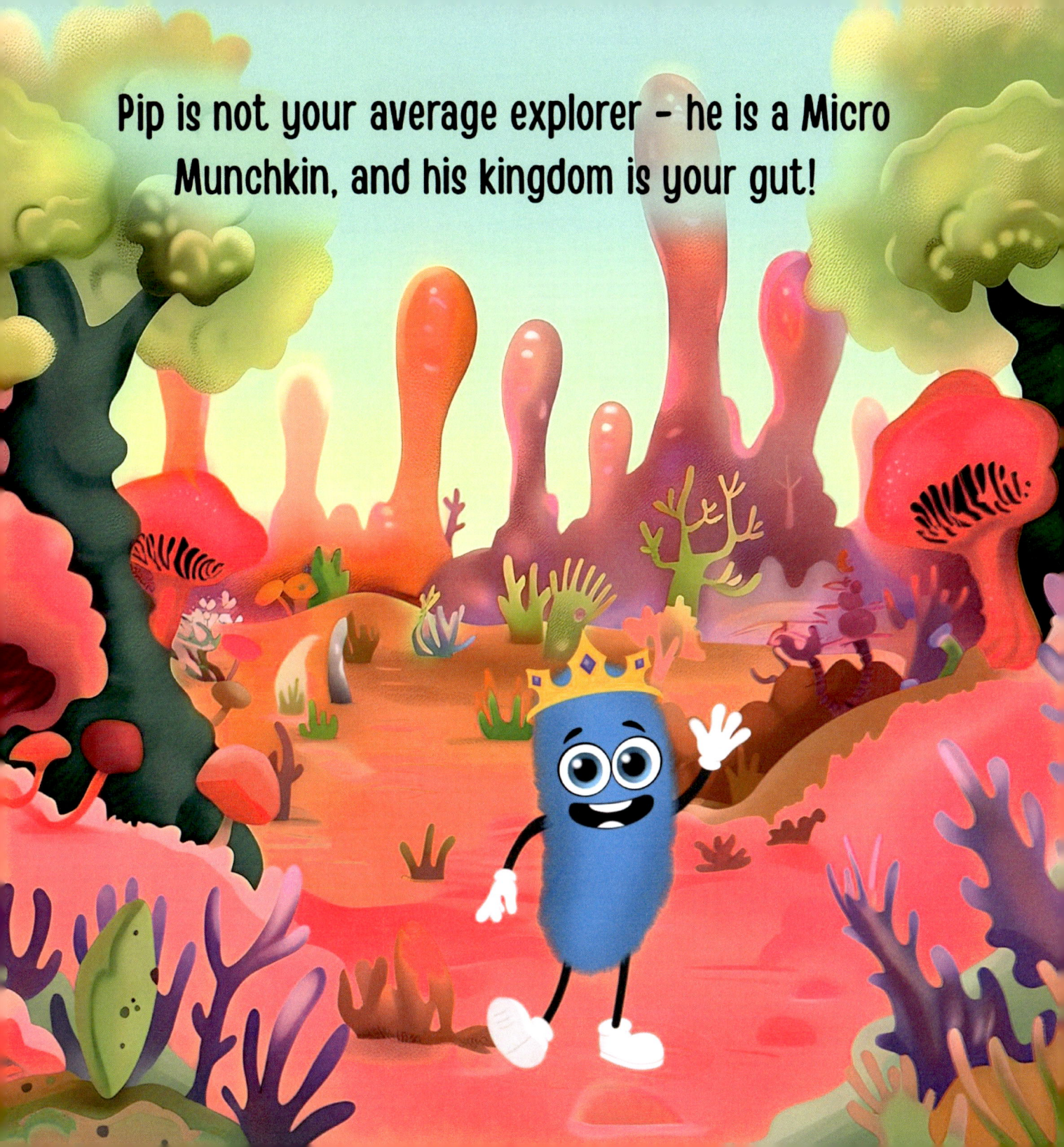

Pip is not your average explorer - he is a Micro Munchkin, and his kingdom is your gut!

Now, your gut is not just a grumbling hole for snacks.

It is a jungle of wiggly tubes called intestines, with streams of yummy food flowing through them.

Pip is a gardner of this amazing world!

His tools are not shovels and rakes, but friendly little fellow Micro Munchkins of all shapes and sizes.

The good Micro Munchkins, called microbes, are the sunshine and rain for Pip's garden.

They munch on fiber from healthy foods like fruits, veggies, and whole grains.

They make vitamins and keep the bad Micro Munchkins, called pathogens, in check, just like gardeners chase away pesky weeds.

Sometimes, sneaky Sugar Goblins creep into Pip's gut garden.

When that happens, they steal the sunshine and rain from good Micro Munchkins, and Pip's garden can't grow properly.

That is when things get grumpy. Your tummy then rumbles and grumbles, and sometimes, it wouldn't feel happy at all.

Luckily, Pip knows just what to do! He will call in his superhero squad - the Veggie Rangers!

The Veggie Rangers are crunchy carrots, juicy oranges, and playful peas.

They are packed with vitamins and fiber, like tiny shields and swords for Pip's garden.

So, every time you choose crunchy carrots over sugary snacks, remember Pip and his gut garden adventure.

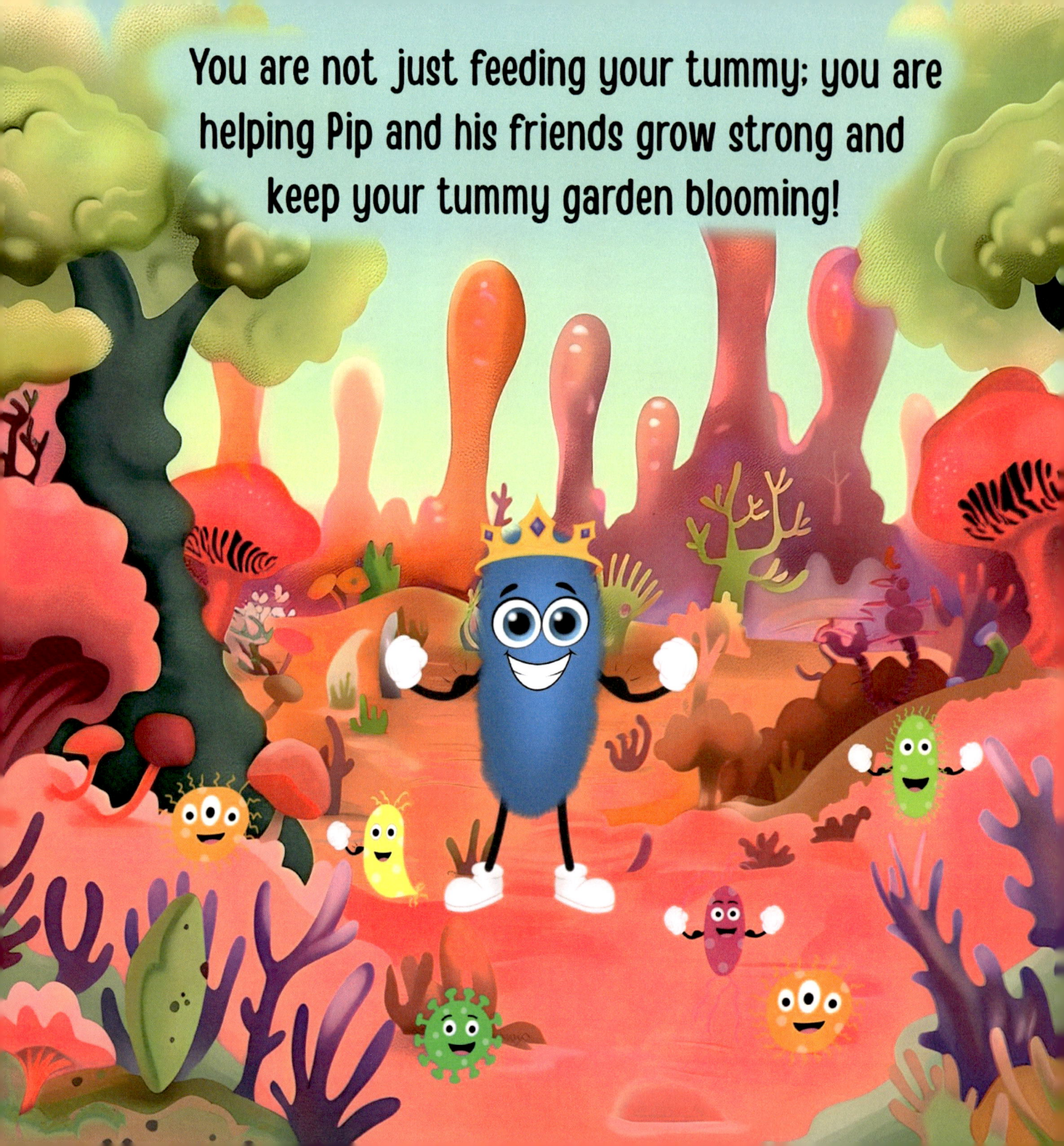
You are not just feeding your tummy; you are helping Pip and his friends grow strong and keep your tummy garden blooming!

Together, you can keep your gut happy and healthy, ready for any adventure that comes your way!

ACTIVITY PAGES

Vitamins and minerals are very important because they help your body not to get sick, they help you to grow big and tall and they also help your organs, and all your tiny cells do their jobs to keep you healthy and strong.

Mum and Dad can have a look at the lists to help all your little friendly Micro Munchkins to be the best little Munchkins they can be.

While mum and dad are creating a shopping list, you can see which of these foods appear in most of the lists – those are the good ones to pick!

VITAMINS

Vitamin A keeps your eyes healthy and helps you to see better in dim light.

- Oily fish
- Eggs
- Yoghurt
- Spinach
- Peppers
- Mango
- Carrots
- Melon
- Pumpkin
- Sweet potato

Vitamin B helps to take in the energy from the food you eat.

- Meat
- Fish
- Nuts (like almonds)
- Eggs
- Beans & Peas
- Sunflower seeds
- Chicken
- Cauliflower
- Spinach
- Broccoli
- Mushrooms
- Bananas

Vitamin C keeps your blood healthy and helps breaks to heal quickly.

- Citrus
- Strawberries
- Peppers
- Tomatoes
- Kiwi fruit
- Carrots
- Leafy green vegetables
- Brussels sprouts
- Broccoli

Vitamin D helps to keep your teeth and bones strong.

- Red meat
- Oily fish
- Eggs

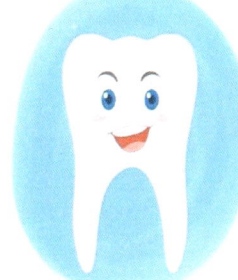

Vitamin E keeps your skin healthy and fight off baddies.

- Nuts and seeds
- Olive oil
- Red peppers
- Leafy green vegetables
- Avocados

Vitamin K helps to heal your cuts and wounds.

- Leafy green vegetables
- Asparagus

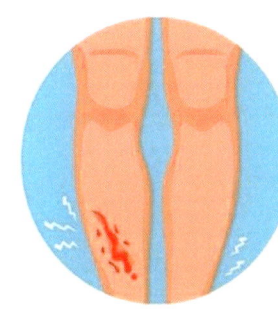

MINERALS

Potassium keeps your muscles and nerves working well.

- Avocado
- Fish
- Seafood
- Banana

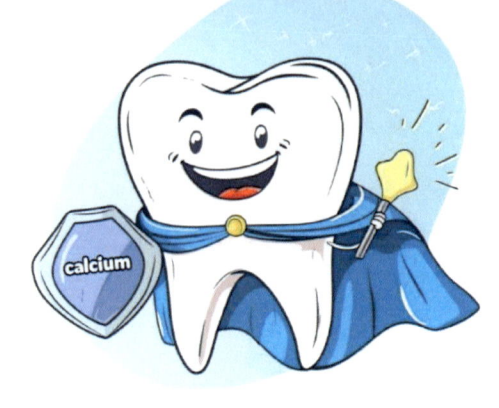

Calcium helps your teeth and bones grow strong.

- Natural yoghurt
- Green vegetables

Iron helps you to not feel tired and sick every day.

- Nuts
- Spinach
- Red meat
- Beans

ABOUT THE AUTHOR

Yvette is a nutritionist with a passion for empowering individuals to achieve their healthiest selves. She believes that teaching children from a young age about nutrition and the importance of gut health will be the necessary shift to increase healthy eating and reduce obesity while keeping children healthy and full of the necessary energy to grow into the magnificent human beings we hope they will become.

www.ingramcontent.com/pod-product-compliance
Lightning Source LLC
Chambersburg PA
CBRC091724070526
44585CB00008B/163